Merry Christmas 2016
for Amos
from

THREE RIVERS PRESS · NEW YORK

BAT DAD

Blake Wilson

A PARODY

Copyright © 2016 by Blake Wilson

Published in the United States by Three Rivers Press, an imprint of the Crown
Publishing Group, a division of Penguin Random House LLC, New York.
crownpublishing.com

Three Rivers Press and the Tugboat design are registered trademarks of
Penguin Random House LLC.

Library of Congress Cataloging-in-Publication Data
Names: Wilson, Blake, author.
Title: BatDad : a parody / Blake Wilson.
Description: New York : Three Rivers Press, 2016.
Identifiers: LCCN 2016004066 | ISBN 9780451495501 (hardback)
Subjects: LCSH: Fatherhood—Humor. | Family—Humor. | BatDad (YouTube Video)
  | BISAC: HUMOR / Topic / Marriage & Family. | FAMILY & RELATIONSHIPS /
  Parenting / Fatherhood.
Classification: LCC PN6231.F37 W55 2016 | DDC 818/.602—dc23 LC record available at https://lccn.loc.
gov/2016004066

ISBN 978-0-451-49550-1
eBook ISBN 978-0-451-49551-8

Printed in the United States of America

Book design by Elizabeth Rendfleisch
Interior art (bubbles/dot pattern): Sabri Deniz Kizil/shutterstock & Mikhail Grachikov/shutterstock
Cover design by Alane Gianetti
Cover photographs: Courtesy of the author; (bubbles) KID_A/shutterstock & P.Jirawat/shutterstock

10 9 8 7 6 5 4 3 2 1

First Edition

WHO WOULD EVER HAVE GUESSED THAT A ROUTINE TRIP TO TARGET WOULD RESULT IN THE GREATEST SUPERHERO WHO EVER LIVED? (*OR AT LEAST THE GREATEST SUPERHERO WHO EVER POSTED VIDEOS TO THE INTERNET.*)

My wife, Jen, and I have four kids under the age of eleven. So a solo outing, just the two of us, is a rare occurrence. But one weekday, there we were at Target picking out a birthday present for one of the kids' friends. (Not quite dinner and a movie, but come on, with four kids we take what we can get.) At the same store a few weeks before, a Batman mask big enough to fit an adult head had caught my eye. And so on this shopping trip, I decided that *I* deserved a little present—what the hell. I bought the mask.

As soon as we got in the car in the parking lot, I put on the mask and started talking like Batman. Jen thought it was pretty silly and stupid, which only egged me on because I will do anything I can to make her laugh. When she did, I knew I was on to something, so I filmed it. I'd been playing around with Vine, where I could make short, easy videos that didn't take a lot of time—something I don't have a lot of with the four kids—and so I posted it there.

But it was when I got home that BatDad was truly born. I was really excited to play this character with the kids and made a bunch more videos that very same day. With the mask on, it made all the day-to-day stuff—the laundry, the homework, the pretend tea parties—a whole new hilarious and fun experience. The kids provided plenty of inspiration for video ideas, and then soon enough they started having their own ideas! Even now, it's hysterical to watch them watching BatDad video compilations; it's almost like they're not watching themselves.

But it turned out they weren't the only ones watching. Places like BuzzFeed and Reddit started taking notice. Fox News and PBS were talking about us. The *Today* show came to our house to film us. The president of the United States told the world he loved what I was doing in *People* magazine! I think what people really like about the videos is that they are these short snippets of everyday life that all parents can relate to—spills, jumping on the couch, the hours it takes to put a kid to bed, a husband being annoying—and see the humor in them in a way they might not in the moment. And many parents have told me that the videos are something they can watch with their kids and have a laugh together. I hope this book has the same effect.

So what's next? Moody teenagers, dating, college? I don't know, but I'll be ready with this $10 mask. I'm having a blast making these videos with my family, and the fact that you all are getting such a kick out of them is honestly the only reason my wife lets me keep making them.

So, on that note . . . *JEN!!!!*

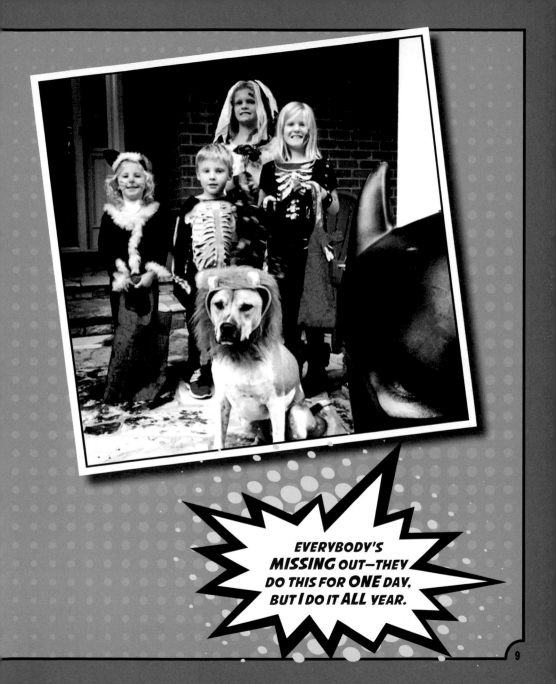

EVERYBODY'S **MISSING** OUT—THEY DO THIS FOR **ONE** DAY, BUT I DO IT **ALL** YEAR.

Name: Sienna   Date: 9-8-15 20

Interview with my parent about his/her job

1. I spoke to _____ mom (and/or) ✓ dad.

2. Where do you work? Wherever I want

3. What do you do there? Make silly videos
in a Batman mask

4. What time do you leave for work? Whenever

5. What time do you get home from work? Whenever

6. What do you like best about your job? _____
Goofing off / Having fun

7. What did you want to be when you were little?
A Turtle

SIENNA
Child's signature

Parent's signature

BATDAD'S STRUGGLE IS REAL. REAL FUN.

ONE OF THESE DAYS, I *REALLY*
NEED TO TURN *AROUND*
AND *CATCH* HIM IN THE ACT.

STAY OUT OF THE CLOSET.
IT'S FULL OF **VILLAINS.** OR NEATLY
FOLDED TOWELS. **BUT** LET'S SAY VILLAINS.
YOU KNOW WHAT? **JUST STAY OUT.**

THEY *FOUND*
MY *WEAKNESS.*
HIGH-PITCHED
SCREAMING.

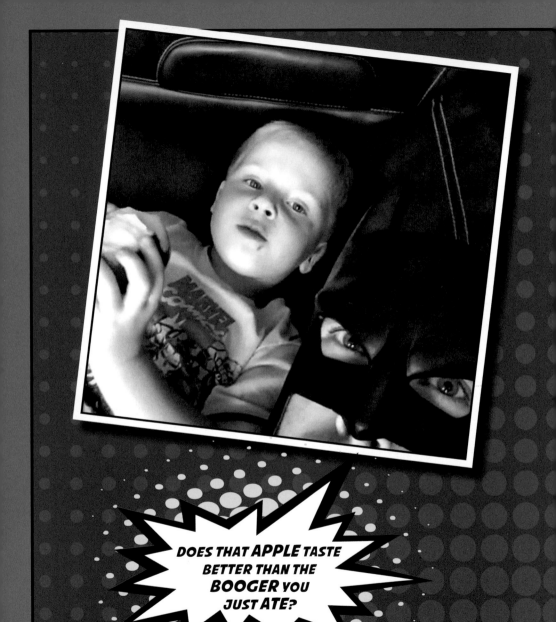

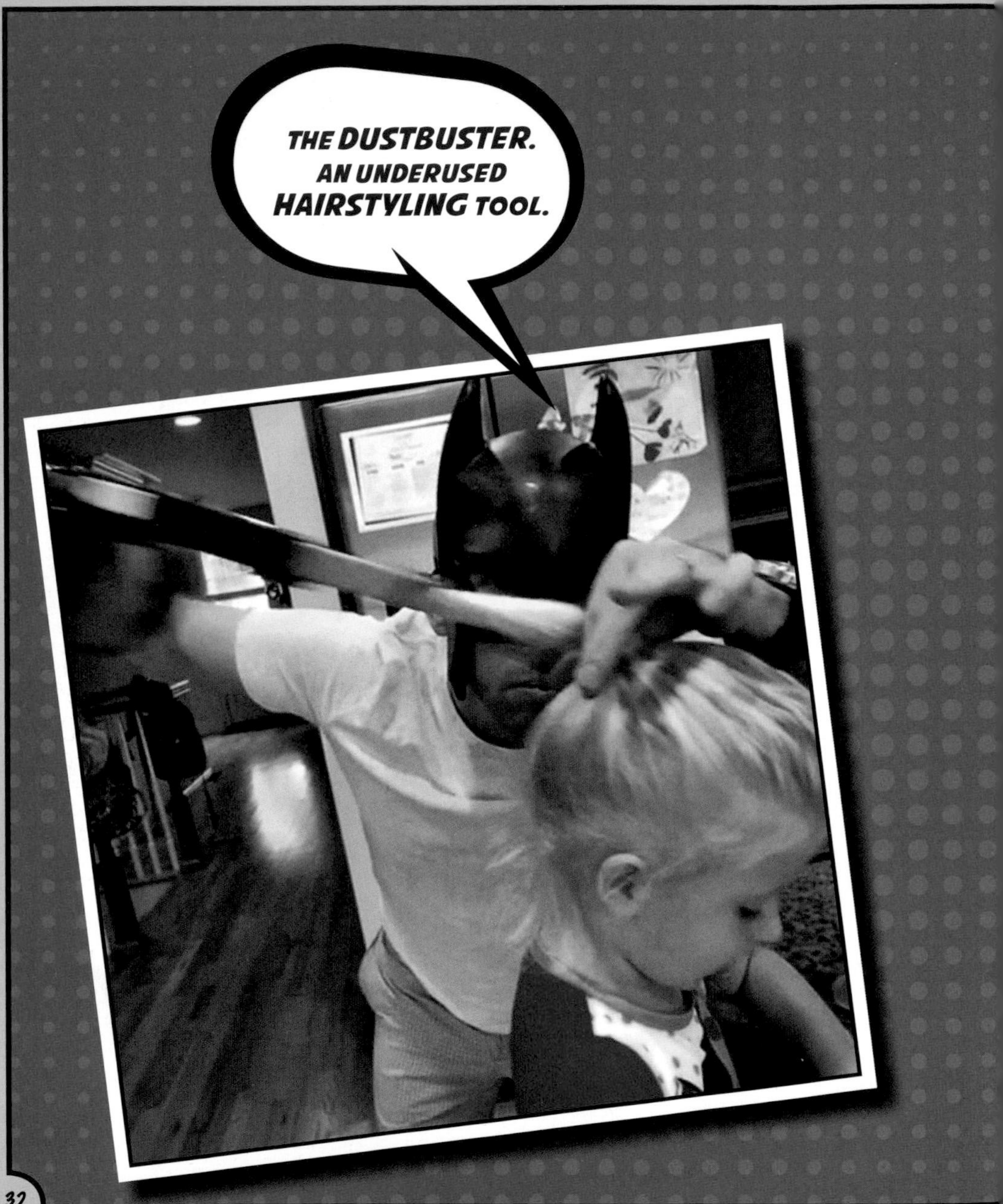
THE DUSTBUSTER. AN UNDERUSED HAIRSTYLING TOOL.

TABLES **ARE** FOR
GLASSES. **NOT** ASSES.

THE **THINGS** WE DO FOR **OUR** DAUGHTERS.

SOMETIMES A BOY **CAN** HAVE TOO MANY SISTERS.

CHILDREN. THEY HIDE **WHERE**
YOU **LEAST** EXPECT THEM TO
BE. BUT WHERE YOU **EXPECT**
FRYING PANS TO BE.

46

PUT IT **UNDER** YOUR PILLOW
AND **WAIT** FOR . . .
THE **BAT FAIRY.**

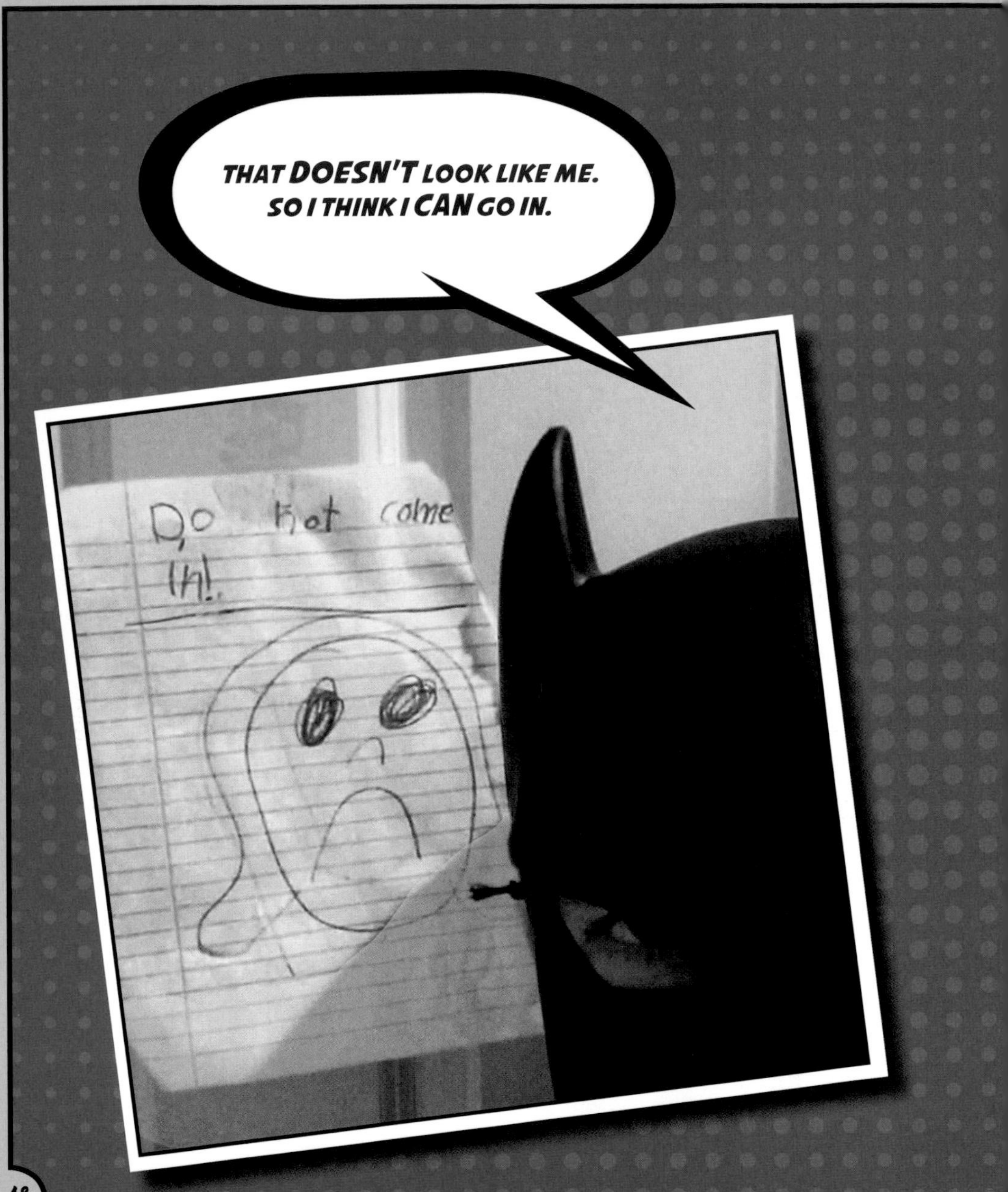
THAT DOESN'T LOOK LIKE ME.
SO I THINK I CAN GO IN.

THESE KIDS GIVE ME A MASKACHE SOMETIMES. I MEAN **ALL** THE TIME.

SMALL **CHILDREN.**
BIG PILES OF LAUNDRY.
HOW IS THIS
PHYSICALLY **POSSIBLE?**

THAT'S A DRESS YOU MADE?
ARE YOU **SURE?**

ONE ORNAMENT IS FINE. BUT NO CHRISTMAS TREE LIGHTS!